YOUR FIRST 50 BOOK REVIEWS

ALLIANCE OF INDEPENDENT AUTHORS

A NOTE ABOUT ALLI
THE ALLIANCE OF INDEPENDENT AUTHORS

This book is one of a number of self-publishing guidebooks and campaign books for authors produced by the Alliance of Independent Authors (ALLi).

If you haven't yet heard of ALLi, it is a global, non-profit association for self-publishing authors. Our mission is ethics and excellence in self-publishing and we bring together thousands of indie authors all over the world who are united behind this mission.

All our profits are reinvested back into the organization for the benefit of our members—and the wider author community.

ALLi is pronounced "ally" (al-eye), and an ally is what we aim to be to self-publishers everywhere. Our name is spelt with a big ALL and small i because our members are like the three musketeers in Dumas's eponymous novel: ALL working for each individual "i", and each for ALL.

ALLi offers members a range of benefits but our real strength is our members, team and advisors, who provide something like the ancient system of craft apprenticeship, with the wisdom of the hive-mind instead of one master.

Our work is fourfold:

A Note About ALLi

- ALLi *advises*, providing best-practice information and education through a Self-Publishing Advice Center that offers a daily blog, weekly livestreams and podcasts, a bookstore of self-publishing guidebooks, and a quarterly member magazine.
- ALLi *monitors* the self-publishing sector through a **watchdog desk**, alerting authors to bad actors and predatory players and running an approved partner program.
- ALLi *campaigns* for the **advancement of indie authors** in the publishing and literary sectors globally (bookstores, libraries, literary events, prizes, grants, awards, and other author organizations), encouraging the provision of publishing and business skills for authors, speaking out against iniquities, and furthering the indie author cause wherever possible.
- ALLi *empowers* independent authors through a wide variety of **member tools and resources** including author forums, contract advice, sample agreements, networking, literary agency representation, and a member care desk.

Headquartered in London, we operate all over the world and at every level, bringing our mission of ethics and excellence in self-publishing to beginner, emerging and experienced authors. Whether you're just starting out, or you're already widely published, ALLi can empower you to make better books, reach more readers, and generate greater profits.

When you join ALLi, you're not just joining an organization, you're becoming part a transformative, self-organising, global author movement. Whether you're self-publishing your first novel or your fiftieth, ALLi is with you every step of the way, with a suite of member benefits that includes free guidebooks, discounts and deals, member forums, contract consultancy, advisory board, literary agency, watchdog and more.

Your membership also supports our advocacy work for indie authors globally, from Alaska to New Zealand and offers access to ALLi's supportive, dynamic community.

A Note About ALLi

If you haven't yet, is it time you joined us?
AllianceIndependentAuthors.org

INTRODUCTION

Encouraging people to publish and share reviews of your book should be a key activity in your author marketing toolbox. Reviews indicate a sense of credibility. They offer social proof—an assurance that other readers have enjoyed the book—and instill confidence about your book in new readers, making them more likely to convert from browsers to buyers.

Social proof is widely considered the bedrock of the purchasing-decision process for today's consumer. Think about your own behavior when you want to book a trip, buy a new car, or reserve a table at a restaurant. If you're like most people, you'll check online reviews of the location, hotel, dealership, food, and venue. Most of us now turn to reviews for help when deciding whether it's worth our time and money to try something new. We even get suspicious if we can't find reviews when looking to make a purchase.

It's the same way with books.

Ten years ago, if you asked authors or publishers about getting book reviews, they probably would've answered in terms of traditional print media and review periodicals. Trade magazines like *Publishers' Weekly* or *The Bookseller*. Literary magazines like *The New Yorker* or *The Times Literary Supplement*. The review sections slotted into the daily

Introduction

and weekend newspapers, radio programs, and TV shows. All these avenues comprised the bulk of their review-generating strategy.

These days, far more book reviews happen online and from regular readers. Instead of professional critics doing the posting, it's largely the audience of readers. And instead of only listening to one authority figure's opinion, many potential readers now prefer to gain a consensus of the opinions of hundreds or thousands of amateurs and "unknowns." Reader reviews on book retailer sites, especially Amazon and Goodreads (which is owned by Amazon), now have a large impact on reader behavior in addition to the critic and book reviews on blogs and podcasts.

This short book is a guide to getting reviews in all these arenas, based on ALLi's best advice and on the experience of our members. Beginners and experienced authors alike can use the strategies that follow to complement whatever you're currently doing to get reviews. No matter your skill and knowledge level, you'll find useful takeaways in this guide.

It's helpful to start with an understanding of some key principles. First, trends and reader habits are constantly shifting. As such, the tools are updated often and sometimes replaced as modern operators create products and services to help indie authors get more reviews. While we have made every effort to provide up-to-date information at the time of writing, some of the tools and processes might have already changed by the time you read this book. But you can still get lots of reviews and advance your author career by following core strategies. We have included those that have stood the test of time and cover most commercial and critical bases to make this text as evergreen as possible.

It's worth mentioning that, when referring to costs, we have translated everything into United States Dollars (USD) unless quoting a source. U.S. currency is widely considered the most universal one for indie authors since the dominant service providers working in the self-publishing arena originate in the US.

In terms of navigation, this book is intended to be read in chronological order. However, those who prefer to jump straight to sections that interest them, without reading the chapters in between,

Introduction

can easily read and comprehend individual chapters without having to flip back to find definitions or understand context. We've also added "Key Takeaways" at the end of every chapter for summation and simplicity. We know authors lead busy lives, so these takeaways were created with that in mind.

Some of the steps for getting reviews require technical knowledge. But if you're not tech savvy, don't worry. We've made every attempt to minimize jargon and complex processes. Though today's book reviews are primarily organized and collected over the internet, most authors who are rocking the reviews scene never considered themselves to be technically minded. Some of the following activities may require skills that you need to develop, but most of the work will be straightforward and only require a basic grasp of how the internet works.

Everyone starts at the beginning. As an organization that has your back, we offer guidance to master current best practices. Examine the advice we offer, then make choices the creative way: trying and testing, experimenting and exploring. When you keep what works for you and drop what doesn't, your process and results will improve.

Most of the strategies in this guidebook will not cost you a lot of time or money, but some will take courage. Fear holds many authors back from taking the first step to get more reviews. This guide will encourage you to simply take one step at a time. Opening your work up to public criticism can be scary but can also be a fruitful endeavor.

Having said that, we urge you not to jump right in to gathering reviews without understanding the rules of the game. Rules and ethical boundaries do exist in this space, and the penalties for breaking them can be dire. If your quest for reviews begins before you understand the code of ethics that many retailers and governments require you to follow, you may inadvertently damage your reputation and career potential as an authorpreneur. As such, it's important that you learn the reviewing rules of each bookselling platform before you invest time and effort into asking readers to post reviews there. You must also know the government laws surrounding how to collect and store reviewer data.

You won't go wrong if your activities related to soliciting book reviews align with ALLi's Ethical Author Code (See Appendix on pg.

Introduction

X.). The Ethical Author Code began as a campaign in late-2014 to promote ethical author behavior and to counter the damage done to our collective reputations by unethical individuals. You'll find more in the pages ahead on the ethics that are paramount to effectively conducting a review-generating activity.

You've accomplished the massive undertaking of putting your book out into the world. Going that extra step to ask for people's opinions and reviews can be daunting. As authors, many of us would rather shy away from the challenge. That's understandable. But we are not just authors; we are publishers. A good author may avoid reviews, but a good publisher seeks them. This guide will help you find the way.

1
START WITH MINDSET

When learning any new skill or practice, adopting the most effective mindset is key. As an indie author, you are an author-publisher, which means you are juggling more than one mindset. You need to be an inner-directed writer, in touch with your innermost thoughts, feelings and ideas and able to hone them into words. And you also need to be an outer-directed publisher, in touch with what readers need and want and how to best encourage them to buy and read your books.

As a writer, you want to produce the best books you can produce. As a publisher, you want to ensure that prospective readers know how good the books are so they will want to buy and read them. You also need to ensure that all strategies to get more reviews for your books are ethical and not misleading—fair to readers, other writers and other players in the bookselling ecosystem, who must not be misled by our natural desire to receive good reviews.

Internalizing this double-mindset will make the strategies in this book easier to accomplish.

Make it your mission to motivate your readers to review your books. Once you do, reviews will start to appear. What's more, you will become less "attached" to the content of reviews, where getting positive reviews causes a dopamine spike of delight, but getting negative ones throws you into a tailspin. Exposing yourself to more reviews lessens this emotional rollercoaster ride.

The mature author-publisher approaches reviews in a spirit of curiosity. What can I take from this feedback? How does it alert me to what I've done well, or what I need to improve. Once you've been through the process a few times, you'll learn to react to both criticism and praise in the same way. Instead of throwing off your day, you will acknowledge them purely as a learning opportunity—a way to become a better author and publisher.

Rather than fixating on reviews, positive or negative, you know they won't derail you, even when readers say cruel or crazy things. You stay connected to that most important item on your to-do list: writing the next book.

In this guide, we have curated what we think are the best tools and actions you can use to grow the number of book reviews you receive, even on a limited time or money budget. You can rely on this book to guide you through the process but it's up to you to bring the positive, committed, and consistent approach that it takes.

Approach the act of growing your book reviews with an enthusiastic but ethical mindset. Follow the lead of the best indie authors and publishers working in publishing today, and you will gain more reviews and, ultimately, sales. Your reviews will remain prominent and provide social proof for your books over the long term. Plus, your ethical and effective author mindset will ensure that you're appreciated by readers and respected by your industry peers.

Key Takeaways

When developing an effective mindset about reviews, you must:

- Think like a publisher who wants to sell books.
- See reviews as a selling and learning tool, rather than something to fear.

- Expose yourself to reviews until you learn not to fixate on their content.
- Work with a strong ethical code to benefit the community and your reputation.

2
TYPES OF BOOK REVIEWS

When looking to build social proof for your book, it's important to know that there are many types of book reviews available to you. Each type serves a different purpose, appeals to a specific type of audience, and offers variable success depending on the genre in which you publish. Knowing the difference is vital because gathering these reviews costs time and money, so you'll want to spend both well. Let's look at the different review options and examine each one.

Generally, book reviews fall into the following categories:

1. Reviews in mass media.
2. Reviews in book trade publications.
3. Reviews by book bloggers.
4. Reviews by readers given an advance copy for review.
5. Reviews by influencers relevant to your genre, free and paid.
6. Organic customer reviews.

Reviews in Mass Media

Mass media reviews in newspapers and magazines were traditionally the only significant way to let people know about books, and they are still highly influential. This is especially the case when you consider the "Review" sections of established publications like *The New York Times* or *The Guardian*. Radio and TV book review and interview programs, like the *Oprah Show* or the *Richard and Judy* book clubs, are also examples of influential mass media reviews.

Reviews in Book Trade Publications

People connected with the publishing industry read book trade publications. Publishers, agents, booksellers, librarians, marketing agencies, and book reviewers all read publications and associated websites like *Publishers Weekly*, *Foreword Reviews*, *Kirkus Reviews*, and *Library Journal*, among others. You can request one of these publications to select your book to be reviewed for free. Getting a review in a book trade publication is often considered one of the best ways to catch the attention of trade distributors and corporate book buyers.

Reviews by Book Bloggers

Book bloggers are avid readers who have developed online followers. You can find them on their own websites, but also on sites like Facebook, Tumblr, and Twitter. They can be very influential in creating fan buzz about books. Some book bloggers reach thousands of readers every week. In recent years, as blogging has become more competitive, this space has given rise to book vloggers who record videos to review books and upload them to video- and visual-based social media sites like YouTube and Instagram.

Reader Reviews from an Advance Review Copy

An advance review copy, often shortened to "ARCs," are book copies that authors or publishers provide, often for free and prior to publishing, to a select group of readers. They do this in the hope that those early readers will write and publish early reviews once the book launches on online bookstores like Amazon, Apple Books, and

Barnes & Noble. Early reviews can lead to more successful book launches.

Organic Reviews by Online Customers

Reader customer reviews appear on the sales pages of online retailers like Amazon, Apple Books, Goodreads, Google, and Kobo. They are usually submitted by readers who have purchased the book or received an advance review copy (ARC). Once submitted, they are publicly available for anyone to read.

These reader reviews on sites like Amazon and Audible provide extremely influential social proof, especially for impulse purchases. A reader could choose to buy or not buy a book based on the quality, quantity, and star average of customer reviews associated with the book. In fact, many authors argue that they are almost as influential as the front cover.

There are many good reasons why reader reviews are front of mind for most authors:

- Research shows they influence readers' decisions to buy.
- They are public and evergreen (unless the retailer decides to remove them).
- They are accessible, democratic, and offer a consensus of reader opinions.
- They are linked to retailer algorithms, so getting them gives a book more exposure.

Free Editorial Reviews

Influencers, celebrities, experts, and authors offer free editorial reviews for the right book and audience. Publishers display these reviews, sometimes called endorsements, on the front or back cover and inside the front matter of their books. They are often also included in the "editorial reviews" section of their Amazon sales page with a heading such as "Praise for [author]."

You can obtain free editorial reviews by reaching out to a specific list of influential people and outlets relevant to your genre, providing them with a free copy, and asking for a review or an endorsement quote. This can work well when you're asking well-known authors who might be both known to your readers and interested in having their name and "author of [book title]" appear where your readers can discover them. This can be nice win-win for both authors.

Paid Editorial Reviews

Authors, both indie and traditional, can and do pay for editorial reviews. This is not paying a fee to receive a good review which is unethical, according to ALLi's Ethical Author policy. Good editorial review services provide *objective* reviews for a fee. Among the reputable fee-for-review services are: *Foreword Clarion Reviews, BlueInk, Kirkus Indie Reviews, Chanticleer Book Reviews,* and *Publishers Weekly's BookLife.*

As with every other aspect of publishing, there are disreputable review services out there. ALLi offers details on the reputable ones so you can sidestep fraudsters and maintain ethical but effective author business practices. For ALLi's list of services, reviewed and rated, check ALLi's Watchdog Desk on SelfPublishingAdvice.org/best-self-publishing-services. If you're an ALLi member, check out the ALLi Partner database, where you can contact good services directly and receive member discounts.

In the chapter, "Free Versus Paid Editorial Reviews," we help you to differentiate between the good and the bad and to decide whether pursuing paid reviews might be right for you.

The Right Reviews for You and Your Book

Which type of reviews you choose to pursue should depend entirely on the genre of your books, your goals as an author, the financial implications for your business and your ethical stance.

There are as many types of platforms to pursue reviews as there are types of reviews themselves.

As in so much in the book business, Amazon is the dominant

player in the review space, and getting lots of positive reviews there will provide a significant benefit to most authors. We examine Amazon reviews in detail but there are many other platforms to choose from, and also your own website, social media, booksellers, newspapers, blogger sites, and more.

This guidebook offers details about all avenues available to you so you can create the review strategy that best suits you.

Key Takeaways

When seeking reviews, it's important to note:

- Each type of review serves a different purpose.
- Each review type and platform appeals to a specific type of audience.
- Gathering reviews costs time money, so pursue the right ones for you and your book.
- Reviews and endorsements confer credibility and social proof.
- Consider reputable editorial review services to augment your review strategy.

3
USING ADVANCE REVIEW COPIES (ARCS)

Advance Review Copies (ARCs) are digital or physical copies of a book a publisher distributes to generate buzz and get early reviews on their books. Providing a finished but not-yet-published book to a group of readers for free, along with a request that they write and post a review, is a standard strategy for indie authors—arguably, the most prominent. It can be a time-consuming but rewarding activity.

There are rules around ARC distribution and many authors consider them an essential part of their business model. Individual author opinions differ on this matter. In this chapter we will explore two case studies from ALLi members: a historical novelist who used ARCs with some success and an opinion piece arguing that readers receiving free books in exchange for reviews is unethical.

The ARC Team

One of the many benefits of being an indie author is that you can move faster through the publishing process than if you had a traditional publishing contract. It's worth remembering, though, that one reason why trade publishers take so long to publish is that they build review and promotion activities into their launch process before making the book commercially available. It's a strategy that works well to build momentum for a book *before* it is published.

You can use this strategy, too. One way is to produce and distribute print and/or electronic ARCs to pre-publication readers with the aim of bringing in early reviews and quotable testimonials for marketing purposes. If you are willing to restrain yourself long enough between completing your book and taking it to market, you can benefit from the ARC process.

Many leading indie authors who sell in huge numbers put a dedicated ARC strategy at the heart of their business. Dan Parsons, ALLi's book production manager says,

> Most successful indie authors deem their ARC team to be among their most valuable assets. Compiling an ARC team should be a priority for a new author, because you can contact them as often as you want once you've built the list – a strategy that will save you time and money during future releases.
>
> It's also a good way to keep your most avid readers engaged. Some digital giveaways and a monthly email is a small price to pay for having a personal army of superfans on hand to review and promote your new releases.

An Argument Against ARCs

In contrast to Dorah Blume, and frontline independent authors like Mark Dawson, Joanna Penn and many others, ALLi author member Mark Horrell, considers such dedicated use of an ARC team poses a controversial question about the practice of giving away free books in exchange for reviews. In the following article, he suggests that offering ARCs may break the spirit of the law, even if the potential reviewer is not pressured into reviewing.

There has been much discussion about Amazon reviews. It seems that a lot of indie authors have seen five-star reviews disappearing with no explanation. This is infuriating; we don't have big marketing budgets, and word-of-mouth is one of our most important ways of getting new readers.

I've followed these discussions from the sidelines. I'm one of the lucky authors who has hundreds of favorable Amazon reviews, yet—yet as far as I'm aware—hasn't seen a single one disappear. Perhaps I should be worried that I will be next, but I'm relaxed.

Almost all of my reviews are organic, written by complete strangers who have picked up my books, enjoyed them, and been kind enough to leave feedback for others. I'm extremely grateful to these people because they owe me nothing.

How Do I Get These Reviews?

I put a friendly request at the back of my books. When I blog about my writing, I leave a note at the end of the post asking readers to kindly leave a review.

I don't ask friends and family to post reviews, and as far as I'm aware, only one or two of them ever have.

The ARC Route to Reviews

Another thing I don't do is send out advance reader copies (ARCs) of my books.

Some indie authors take this practice very seriously and assemble substantial 'ARC teams' of engaged readers who are happy to post a review in return for an advance copy.

I don't have an ARC team for two reasons. In my opinion, it's a breach of Amazon's guidelines. Secondly, I consider it to be unethical.

Let's start with the first of these reasons, because it's more clear cut. In their review policy, Amazon gives some examples of customer reviews that they don't allow. Two of these are:

1. A customer posts a review in exchange for financial reward.

2. A family member of the product creator posts a five-star review to help boost sales.

This seems clear enough. If you have reviews that are either of these things, then you can have no complaints if the review disappears. I believe Amazon considers a free copy to be a financial reward.

Many of these reviews are easy to spot. If, for example, a book receives a lot of five-star reviews on the same day that it goes on sale, then it's likely the readers received advance copies (not many people can read a book that quickly).

It may seem like a natural kindness to give someone a book and ask them politely to leave *honest* feedback, but if you do this systematically, there comes a point when it's no longer honest but deceitful.

Consider the Reader's Perspective

To understand this point, it's necessary to put ourselves in our readers' shoes. This should be easy for us to do; after all, we are readers too and consumers of services that benefit from unbiased feedback.

Let me give some examples of how reviews and opinions in exchange for financial reward can become deceitful.

Suppose you visit a restaurant because it received a large number of positive reviews on TripAdvisor. The restaurant turns out to be pretty average. When it's time to pay your bill, the waiter returns with an iPad and the offer of 10 percent off your bill if you post a review. It may be tempting to claim your discount, but you've just visited an average restaurant because other people succumbed to that very same temptation.

A guidebook writer visits a hotel and is treated like royalty because the owner knows they've come to review it. When an ordinary traveler arrives the following year on the strength of a review they saw in the guidebook, they receive a completely different standard of service.

As a sideline to my books, I also write an outdoor blog. It's common practice for outdoor retailers and brands to invite bloggers like me to review equipment and clothing. There are many outdoor bloggers who are only too happy to receive free clothing in return for a review. But these reviews can never be completely honest because the blogger knows that the brand will stop sending free clothing if they write negative reviews (in the same way that you will probably drop readers from your ARC team if they do likewise).

Although I sometimes review outdoor gear in a light-hearted way, I have never accepted free clothing. But I also review mountaineering books, and in the past I've accepted requests from authors and publishers to review theirs.

I don't do this anymore.

I found it very difficult to post an honest review if I didn't like the book. These authors were my friends on social media, and I didn't want to upset them.

Fake News, Fake Reviews

We live in an era of fake news and reviews, and I could give many other examples, but hopefully you get the idea.

I believe it's in our interest as readers and consumers to promote honesty and objectivity. Reviews in exchange for free books are fake reviews.

Amazon is quite right to remove them.

I hope I'm not the only indie author who feels this way.

— MARK HORRELL, ALLi AUTHOR MEMBER, MOUNTAINEERING DIARIST, BLOGGER, AND AUTHOR

ARCs for Endorsements

US novelist Dorah Blume used her ARC in a different way, to acquire a high-profile endorsement for her novel, Botticelli's Muse. Despite finding it costly and slow, she recommends the strategy. Here's the timeline that unfolded the ace review.

December: I decided I needed confirmation that this writing project I had been working on for years was finally going to be born as a book, so on December 31, with the help of a local

Espresso Book Machine at the Harvard Book Store, I printed up a bound proof of my novel, even though it was from galley proofs that needed more tweaks and a serious proofread.

February: I saw an article in *artnet News* about Sandro Botticelli and sent an FB messenger into cyberspace to editor Sarah Cascone, telling her about my book.

March: After layout changes and limited proofreading, I generated another bound proof that still needed a final proofread. I ordered 25 bound books from a book printer (approx. $8 a copy).

I sent two copies of the still-not-fully-proofread-bound-proof as ARCs to *Publishers Weekly* through BookLife, their indie author publishing forum. They requested a three-month lead time BEFORE publication.

Sarah sent me an FB message that she wanted to know more about the book. I offered to send her a copy. On March 27, she gave me her address and I sent her one of the 25 ARCs on March 31.

April: Sarah told me she had received the book and was looking forward to taking a look at it. BookLife acknowledged receipt of my book. I ordered two more sample bound copies: one from KDPP and one from IngramSpark. My book has close to 90 black and white spot illustrations in it, and IngramSpark did the better job.

May: I sent a handwritten card to Sarah to see if she had looked at the book, and asked that if she had liked it, would she consider writing a blurb.

BookLife told me they were considering my book for a *Publishers Weekly* review, but that there were no guarantees it would be reviewed.

June: Sarah wrote that she had read the book and that it was "impressive" and that she would like to write a blurb if it wasn't too late. By now I had a new proof, finally proofread and ready to go to press, but I wanted that blurb to put it on the back cover.

Sarah's excellent blurb came in. She suggested she might also want to interview me around the release date. All this communication was on Facebook Messenger. I put it on the back cover and ordered fourteen copies from IngramSpark.

Sarah asked for a high-resolution copy of the book cover so that *Botticelli's Muse* could be added to the *artnet News* summer reading list. I sent out the 7 Mb file immediately through FB Messenger.

The link to the *artnet News* article "15 Scintillating Art Books to Read on the Beach This Summer" featuring my book came in and, of course, I was ecstatic and added it to my author website and my Facebook accounts.

July: BookLife sent me a congratulatory email saying that they had decided to review the book in the coming weeks and that it would be a *Publishers Weekly* review.

— Dorah Blume, US Novelist

There's no doubt that Blume's launch complicated by her wish to send ARCs to selected readers and give them time to respond. Admittedly, these efforts slowed down the launch, but they cultivated buzz, using ARCs in a way that aligned with traditional publishing practices that have been considered ethical for decades. Dorah's book got a coveted blurb quote and extra exposure for the book around release month.

We checked in with Dora for an update and she confirmed that, over time and as expected, her strategy led to more sales, reviews, and word-of-mouth.

Follow the Rules for Kindle Unlimited Reviews

As far as the ALLi's Ethical Author policy allows the provision of free books through ARC teams and we will refer to that methodology throughout this book. Do also consider Amazon's take on the matter. It's easy to fall into potential pitfalls when it comes to ARCs and Amazon's Kindle Unlimited (KU) review policies.

KU is Amazon's subscription reading program, requiring authors and publishers to enrol their book in their exclusive KDP Select program. While ALLi's advice is avoid exclusivity and publish widely across platforms and territories, some authors have legitimate reasons for choosing to enrol one or more books in KDP Select.

If you want your book to be available through KU, be aware that there are specific rules related to ARCs. In a 2019 response to an ALLi query, Amazon's customer service support replied:

> All content made exclusive to Amazon through the KDP Select program must remain for sale on our site only. You cannot make it available free or for purchase in digital e-book format anywhere else, including publishing the content of your book on your website, blogs, etc. However, you may choose to make up to 10 percent of your book available on other sites as a sample (for example, NetGalley), as well as continue to distribute your book in physical format, or in any format other than a digital e-book. (Ten percent is roughly the length of the Kindle Free reading sample.)
>
> — AMAZON CUSTOMER SUPPORT

KDP Select's terms and conditions on exclusivity are short and very clear. Once a book has been enrolled in KDP Select in order to make it available through KU, you can only provide a sample as an ARC, not the whole book.

Does this mean a wrench has been thrown into your ARC strategy? Not necessarily if you confine your ARC distribution to *before* publication. Line up your reviews, publish, give ARC readers a couple of days to get their reviews up there and only *then* enrol the book in KDP Select.

Reviewer Databases

For new authors, in particular, gathering reviews can feel like a vicious circle. You need fans and sales to get reviews but reviews to get sales and fans and not everyone can pull together on a big ARC team in the early stages of their author business. Thankfully, there are companies that have positioned themselves to help overcome this obstacle, including *Author Marketing Club, Book Tribune, Happy Book Reviews, Hidden Gems, Net Galley* and more.

These services offer access to databases of readers that they have built over time. So, if you're struggling without an ARC team, this might be a good alternative. Again, for a full list of services, reviewed and rated, check ALLi's Watchdog Desk on SelfPublishingAdvice.org/best-self-publishing-services. If you're an ALLi member, check out the ALLi Partner database, where you can contact good services directly and receive member discounts.

They all operate in a similar way, albeit at different price points. They provide review copies to readers who have expressed an interest in writing book reviews. These readers aren't obliged to write reviews but many do. They appear as customer reviews, and should not to be confused with the services who organise editorial reviews, covered in the last chapter.

Each of these reviewer databases has different reader demographics, and your genre, cover and content will influence the outcome greatly. One person might get 30 glowing reviews for $50 while another might get 20 poor reviews, or none at all. Testing your options is the best way to find out which work for you. Do your research and take your time if you're considering a service of this type.

Take a Balanced View

Distributing ARCs has clear benefits to authors. But while some authors like Dorah Blume would consider her strategy to be completely ethical and in line with traditional publishing practices, others like Mark Harrell suggest that this practice should be eradicated altogether. What's notable from his case study, in addition to his outlier opinion, is that you don't need ARCs to get lots of favorable reviews.

As an indie author and the creative director of your author business, you must weigh both sides of the argument and decide for yourself.

Key Takeaways

When it comes to using ARCs:

- Some authors use ARCs to gain customer and editorial reviews from traditional media outlets to great success.
- Other authors believe that Amazon is entitled to remove ARC-prompted reviews because they are in breach of its terms of service.
- Amazon rules state that you must not distribute more than 10% of your book for free when in Kindle Select.
- You don't need ARCs to gain lots of positive reviews, but using them can help you kickstart and build your author business.
- It's important to maintain ethical practices if you choose to distribute ARCs. ALLi's Ethical Author policy (see appendix) can help guide you towards an ethical framework that's right for you.

4

AMAZON CUSTOMER REVIEWS

Amazon is the biggest bookseller on the planet. Between its main website, which dominates the much of the world's e-book and print markets, and Audible, the most valuable audiobook seller on earth, it's a true global juggernaut. As a result, building reviews on its platforms can make a huge difference to the fate of an author's titles.

Reviews aren't the only factor that contribute to sales on Amazon, but they do have an impact. And those who build systems to garner positive reviews experience the full force of this effect. How these authors do this, and the scalability of their operation, is key to the success of their brand and rewards them handsomely.

Know Your Reviewers

If you're new to publishing, you may think that unknown authors get most of their reviews from family and friends, and then any extras are entirely organic, the number of which grows as the author establishes a fanbase. However, that assumption is incorrect. Successful indie authors and publishers alike typically approach Amazon with a solid review-generating strategy that involves anywhere between a few dozen and hundreds of reviewers to ensure that their book gets enough reviews to convert browsers into readers.

Through longterm smart effort, front-running authorpreneurs can generate as many as 1,000 honest reader reviews on Amazon and other outlets, within the first month of a book's release, all of which improve their social proof, drive recommendations, and result in hundreds of unit sales a day. To make this possible, they form close bonds with their core reviewers (usually called an ARC team) and keep in constant contact.

It's crucial to identify and understand your reviewers to see this type of success. Not only do the savviest authors know how to identify their ideal readers, but they also know what to say and how to say it in order to coax them into reviewing, and how to nurture their relationships so it strengthens with every book.

They also know that Amazon is the biggest seller of books and where the reviewing ecosystem is most developed. Amazon reviewers are part of a reviewer subculture that authors who want to increase their reviews can explore, research and understand.

Be Ethical for Long-Term for Success

The right sort of positive reviews can generate impressive sales figures and provide a well-earned confidence boost. Negative ones, meanwhile, can ruin your career momentum and send you spiralling into a pit of anxiety. The content of your Amazon reviews, however, is not the only issue you have to consider.

In the "sock-puppet" scandal of 2012, certain authors were found to be manipulating the system for their own gain. They created fake online personas to write positive reviews on their own work and negative reviews on their competitors' books. Understandably, Amazon cracked down, but not necessarily in a nuanced way that only impacted those at fault.

Here is some background on the scenario from John Doppler, ALLi's Self-Publishing Services Watchdog:

In August 2012, several prominent authors admitted publicly to buying fraudulent reviews. The media latched on to the story, and the ensuing scandal prompted Amazon to overhaul enforcement of its rules governing customer reviews.

Unfortunately, the algorithms they used and the policies they implemented were overly aggressive, leading to the erasure of thousands of legitimate reviews.

Authors voiced their concerns, and Amazon responded. They formally clarified their policy to state that authors may review other authors' work, provided they did not have a personal or financial relationship.

In 2015, we faced a new upheaval. Another Amazon initiative to curb review fraud purged tens of thousands of reviews that violate the Customer Review Guidelines, along with many legitimate ones.

However, this time we saw a significant, troubling difference in the way authors chose to react.

Inflammatory blog posts sprung up across the internet, filled with histrionic wailing about "censoring my passion for the written word," and "crossing an ethical line of unfathomable proportions," or spouting misinformation about "draconian new policies" which had actually been in place for years.

Dubious advice about disconnecting your social media accounts proliferated. Some authors fumed about deleted reviews, failing to disclose their own involvement in prohibited review exchanges.

Other authors still propagate these rants and rumors without considering the validity of the claims. Worse still, many do so in full view of their readers.

Yet, for all its seeming indifference, Amazon is not an immovable object. Policy adjustments made in the wake of the 2012 review purge showed that Amazon is not oblivious to our calls for reform. We can persuade the corporate giant to adjust its practices.

— JOHN DOPPLER, ALLi WATCHDOG

The sock-puppet scandal is not unique. As long as there have been ways to abuse the system to maximize a book's chance of success have existed, individuals have opted for such underhanded tactics. However, heed this lesson that working in this way doesn't help your long-term career prospects.

Loopholes can work for a while, but retailers stamp them out eventually. By living in a morally grey area that "technically" follows the rules but isn't ethical, you run the risk of angering peers and losing credibility among your readers, all of which can undo the progress made by your review-generating practices.

So how do you ensure long-term success on Amazon? In 2018, The Alliance of Independent Authors founder and director Orna Ross spoke about the reviews issue in a public interview (available on YouTube: https://youtu.be/tz-E1vDC20A) with Amazon's Darren Hardy, the UK manager for Kindle Direct Publishing, to get some clarity on this issue. In response to her questions, he responded:

> We don't want to get drawn into a detailed conversation about guidelines and decisions because there are people who are looking to abuse those guidelines.
>
> Given the number of books that are published on the platform, it's not scalable for us to reveal every instance of what we've spotted and what we're trying to do about it.
>
> We did have some technical problems. We've sorted those out now and as far as we know those problems haven't repeated.
>
> Like any business, when you create something which is very successful, there's a small percentage of people that look to distort the rules in some ways and cheat the system. We've been working very hard to make sure that legitimate authors are not penalized.
>
> — DARREN HARDY, UK's MANAGER OF KINDLE DIRECT PUBLISHING

Hardy's advice is clear and aligns with ALLi's: you must follow the community guidelines to the letter. Retailers take a dim view on system abuse.

Will bypassing questionable tactics mean making slower progress? In some cases, yes. But it will make continuous success more possible. It will also minimize the impact of setbacks when retailers use heavy-handed tactics to retroactively correct system abuse, eradicate abusers, and plug the gaps these abusers have exposed. You'll still be affected when massive updates occur—almost everyone sees the impact—but you'll weather the storm much more effectively than those who thought they could cut corners to build their reviews.

In 2019, Amazon again suspended the reviewing rights of many would-be reviewers, removing their past reviews while they worked to verify their authenticity. Alas, the unethical behavior of some members of the author community has had an adverse effect on all, as the scale and impact of Amazon's clean-up process was also felt by those who have always behaved ethically. Many ALLi author members report that reviews come in more slowly today, even for books whose sales are healthy.

We will explore how you can work effectively within the rules of Amazon KDP's review policy and ALLi's Ethical Author Policy in upcoming chapters. For now, just know that it's up to each of us in the author community to uphold public confidence in the reader review system.

Inviting Amazon Reviews

Theo Rogers, a top Amazon reviewer and author of *How to Get Good Reviews on Amazon*, has written at length on this topic on the ALLi Self-Publishing Advice blog. After thousands of hours talking with Amazon reviewers, getting inside their heads, and learning what makes them tick, Rogers has also spent as many hours observing the carnage that so often takes place on Amazon's forums. He claims that understanding reviewers and how to talk to them is fundamental to gaining their support. Knowing this, he's developed a deep insider's knowledge of the reviewing subculture that's grown up on Amazon's website.

He's witnessed a lot of authors and other would-be sellers repeat the same mistakes in their dealings with that subculture that more often than not ruin their chances of success. He explains:

> There's a definite reviewer subculture on Amazon. It has its own very definite ideas about what is and is not acceptable behavior, especially on the part of authors... Authors [must]... approach reviewers in a way that the reviewers themselves consider appropriate, and which will result in positive rather than negative attention.
>
> — THEO ROGERS, *HOW TO GET GOOD REVIEWS ON AMAZON*

A reviewer who posts a review is doing you a huge favor by taking time to read your book as well as the time to write a considered review. Remember to be polite and appreciative throughout the process.

Being authentic, honest and ethical is essential to stoking the fires of passion among the right reviewers—many of whom proactively promote their favorite authors. You shouldn't pay Amazon reviewers, and reviewers shouldn't make money from their reviews (post identified affiliate links to the books they review on their own website is the exception).

Trawling the review sections of books that are similar to yours on Amazon is one way to find reviewers. You can also search Amazon's list of top reviewers. Top reviewers are prolific review writers. Identify top Amazon reviewers and offer to send them a free review copy of your book. You can find a list of Amazon's top reviewers here.[1]

Use the steps for a good pitch outlined in "Getting Reviews" chapter. Amazon, other authors, reviewers, and readers consider this method of approaching a reviewer perfectly ethical and acceptable.

Harness the Amazon "Helpful" Button

All authors want positive reviews, but at some point you will get a negative review, and that review might appear at the top of your review section on Amazon. This is irritating but inevitable. Fortunately, there is a way to minimize the impact of a prominently placed bad review.

One thing you can do is get your ARC team to mark positive reviews as "helpful" and negative ones as "unhelpful." Doing so influences which reviews appear in the "top reviews" section on Amazon. Reviews marked as unhelpful get buried, while the reviews that readers deem helpful remain prominent longer.

Key Takeaways

When trying to get reviews on Amazon, know that:

- Amazon reviews will likely influence your global books sales.
- Contact top Amazon reviewers in your genre to optimize your chances on Amazon.
- Have your ARC team mark positive reviews on Amazon as "helpful" to give your best reviews more exposure.
- Individuals who use unethical review tactics eventually face consequences.
- Collecting reviews ethically leads to more reliable long-term success.

---

1. https://www.amazon.com/reviews/top-reviewers.

5
GETTING CUSTOMER REVIEWS

Most successful authors agree that customer reviews have a bigger impact on their long-term sales than any other kind. The principle behind this mentality is simple: most readers get their books from retailer websites. As shoppers, they're influenced to buy books that have both a high average rating and a large number of reviews. Lots of favorable customer reviews is fundamental to success.

The best way to receive more customer reviews is to build strong relationships with readers and motivate them to support you by publishing a review. Building such reader relationships will also help you build a base of fans who will buy every book you write, post reviews about them, and refer your work to their family and friends.

Make it a mission to get these readers invested in your success and they will advance your author career. Doing so costs time rather than money. It means doing some creative thinking, with a positive attitude and determined approach in hand. It also means working out a review-generating process that supports your aims and is sustainable over time. These are strategies within the reach of all authors, as we outline throughout this book and across all platforms.

Pitch to the Right Audience

Targeting the right audience as you seek reviews is essential. Not all efforts to gain reviews will work for every audience. Your genre and your book itself will naturally appeal to a specific kind of reader, so leaning into those readers will make the whole process easier, save you time, and deliver better results

Be focused and purposeful to avoid sabotaging your own efforts. Free giveaways that promote your book to readers who wouldn't normally be interested might result in downloads, but those readers are less likely to appreciate or even read your book. That means they're also less likely to post a positive review. Those who do are more likely to leave bad reviews—not because there's anything wrong with the book, it's just that it doesn't match their preferred reading choice.

Casting a wide net and playing the numbers game doesn't work when seeking reviews. In fact, less is often more. Yes, we'd all love lots of reviews, but it's the *quality* that matters. It's better to have ten five-star reviews than fifty one-star ratings! Create an on-genre cover for your book and use honest sales copy to attract the right sort of readers. Narrowing your focus will result in better reviews, which will lead to more sales and positive reviews in the future.

Pitch the Right Way

Do your research about who reviews books like yours. Approaching them is a productive exercise. Identify potential reviewers across all platforms and offer to send them a free review copy of your book. Check each reviewer's profile to make sure they typically read your genre for best results. If the reviewers make their email addresses or social media profiles publicly available, it means they're happy for authors and publishers to approach them.

The structure of a good review request email, letter, or social media message goes like this:

1. Subject line.
2. Introductory tailored paragraph: *I am writing to you because*

(e.g. *you reviewed a similar book [title]/you seem to be interested in [subject]), and I thought you would be interested in reviewing my book that follows a similar theme.*
3. Explain what your book is about—this can be a modification of your blurb.
4. Offer links where they can access their ARC (advance review copy). Consider using a service like ProlificWorks.com or BookFunnel.com where you can provide sample chapters and/or the full manuscript. If you also have a website or webpage, you can provide that link as well.
5. Requested deadline. If your book hasn't launched yet, you'll want to share the publication date. Also, if it's an endorsement request (see "Free Versus Paid Editorial Reviews"), you'll want to provide at least four weeks' notice. Six to eight is probably better.
6. Provide links where they can post their review, if you have them.
7. End with a line about suggested text that reviewers can include in their review to ensure they adhere to a retailer's terms of service: *If you do post a review, please include this phrase: "I received a free review copy of this book."*

Behave professionally, openly, and helpfully. Make a strong but brief case for why each reviewer should read and review your book. Then wait patiently for their response. Do not pressure them or impose a deadline (remember, it's a *requested deadline* from the list above). If they do review your book, whatever their verdict, thank them sincerely and politely.

Ask for Reviews in Your Book

Including a review request in your e-book or print book is also a good way to collect customer reviews. By doing so, you catch readers' attention when they are most receptive to a review request, immediately after finishing your book. Include a request in your book's end matter that explains why reviews are important and why you would appreciate an online review. Many of your readers will be happy to help you.

This tactic is particularly effective for e-books, where you can embed links that take the reader directly to the reviews page for your book on whatever site you want to target. Where you send them is up to you, whether it's Amazon, your website, or any other retailer

To get your Amazon review link, for example, you can either create an Amazon link to your book using your ASIN or ISBN as follows, replacing "YOUR_ASIN" with your actual ASIN or "ISBN10" with your actual ten-digit ISBN:

https://www.amazon.com/review/create-review?asin=YOUR_ASIN
https://www.amazon.com/review/create-review?asin=ISBN10

YOUR BOOK WON'T BE ASSIGNED AN ASIN UNTIL YOU PUBLISH, MEANING you'll need to publish your e-book version without a link first then refresh your interior file and re-upload it once you've included the link. However, if you purchased your ISBN beforehand, you should be able to include this link in advance. Anyone clicking on the links you include in your back matter will be sent to the Amazon review form for your title. This works for regional stores as well and can be used with universal links like SmartURL.

You can also use a link redirector if you want to provide a neater link or customize the process. On WordPress, for example, you could use a plugin like Pretty Links or Safe Redirect Manager. Or you could put a link in the book like www.example.com/review-book and set up a redirect that sends readers to the review page for your book.

Similarly, you can adapt your e-book or even create multiple versions to send different readers to different stores. As long as you change the copy so that it doesn't mention Amazon, you could link to Kobo in the version you sell in the Kobo store or Apple Books in the version you'll sell on Apple. This process works the same way for every store. It takes extra time, but creating native links and copy for each platform makes those readers feel considered instead of forgotten and improves review conversions. It's totally worth the effort.

If you don't have the time to create multiple versions, you can still create a universal book link that sends readers to a page of retailer logos that they can click to choose their preferred site. Draft2Digital, one of the world's leading e-book self-publishing aggregators, offers a service called Books2Read that helps authors create universal link pages. Their software pulls data from multiple retailers at the push of a button, doing a lot of the work for you if you want to construct one of these pages.

In your book, remember to phrase your review request so that it's clear you're not asking for a lengthy literary appraisal—just a few words that reflect their honest personal opinion. At the time of writing, Amazon's minimum word count for a book review is a mere twenty words, and other retailers will allow even fewer. So, ask your readers, make the task as easy as possible for them, and don't forget to show your appreciation.

Many readers are unaware of how grateful authors are for online reviews. How can they be expected to know this? They aren't engrossed in the world of publishing and bookselling the way we are. If they enjoyed your book, they will almost certainly feel some gratitude toward you and may be glad for the opportunity to interact with you in this way.

Include CTAs Everywhere

Besides asking for customer reviews in your book, you can also request them elsewhere. The more places, the better. ALLi's UK Ambassador and author Debbie Young has great tips on other places to solicit reviews. These include:

- Marketing materials like bookmarks, postcards, and other branded giveaways.
- On your website via a call-to-action widget in the sidebar.
- At the end of discussion sheets, you can offer to virtual book clubs.

- In social media fan groups and public posts.

Share Your Gratitude

Sharing your book reviews on social media, alongside comments on how much they mean to you, has many benefits. Let's say you get a five-star review. By posting it on Twitter, Facebook, or Instagram, it provides social proof to new readers and may encourage fresh sales. It also proves to existing readers that you care about what they say. Many readers like to see their words quoted, so retweeting or posting one of your fan's reviews can turn them into superfans. Not only that, this strategy also reminds other readers to leave a review.

If you're quoting a book blogger's review, share a brief teaser and direct people to the blog to read the review in full. The blogger will appreciate the shout-out. Likewise, if a booktuber makes a video about your book, share that too. Revel in the enthusiasm of your readers in order to generate even more.

Some authors suggest that you should never respond to reviews on Amazon or anywhere else. But if you know a fan who has left a positive review, drop them a private message expressing your appreciation. Thanking them can uplift their day and even lead to more positive reviews on future releases.

Use Retailer Promo Codes

Apple Books and Kobo both encourage readers to leave reviews and reward the authors who get them.

As part of the publishing process, Apple Books offers you 250 promo codes you can use to distribute to reviewers, bloggers, and other PR and media contacts. With a promo code, readers can download your book at no cost. By using these review codes as Apple Books advises, your books show up with higher ratings in the Apple store, increasing your book's visibility and sales.

To obtain your e-book's codes, click the "My Books" tab on the Apple Books dashboard. Select the book for which you would like codes. Click "Promo Codes" and enter the number of codes you want to download. You will then receive an email with the codes and redemption instructions, which you can then provide to each reader who wants to redeem one.

Kobo promo codes work differently, but they are equally effective. Instead of authors distributing the codes themselves, they must apply for a promo in the "Promotions" tab in the Kobo Writing Life dashboard. Kobo will then promote that promo to appropriate readers and ask the author to do the same. Once readers receive their code via email, they can apply it during the checkout process to get a free or discounted copy.

Once you've obtained codes, give them out as quickly as possible. The Apple Books codes expire within a month, and Kobo codes must usually be redeemed within a window of between a day and a week.

It is worth asking your fans who love your work and want you to succeed to post a modified version of their Amazon review on Apple Books and Kobo. These platforms house readers from around the world—many in the primary markets that indies target—and also many others in smaller markets that Amazon doesn't reach, where a few reviews can make a massive difference to exposure.

Aim to Get Consistent

Gathering a steady flow of reviews for your books after launching is vital if you want to see consistent sales. This is something to keep on your weekly to-do list. Some reader reviews arrive organically but, like every other aspect of publishing, consistent effort over time delivers the best results. Using some of the tactics outlined in this book should automate the process somewhat, but ensure you keep broaching the subject with your readers. Evidence suggests that some retailers' recommendation engines factor the recency of reviews into their process. So, if you want to keep selling, keep getting reviews.

Key Takeaways

When pursuing customer reviews, remember to:

- Prioritize them—they impact sales more than any other kind of review.
- Build relationships with readers to get them invested in you and your books.
- Target the right niche of readers to avoid bad reviews and maximize positivity.
- Use your book's back matter to persuade your readers to leave reviews on whatever platform you prefer.
- Include calls-to-action in all of you marketing materials to convert more readers into reviewers.
- Express your gratitude on social media to inspire more reviews.
- Use retailer promo codes to encourage more readers and reviews.
- Take consistent action for more reviews and long-term sales.

6
FREE VERSUS PAID EDITORIAL REVIEWS

Editorial reviews usually come from outlets other than customers. They are the review quotes that you are proud to splash on your cover, in your front matter, on your sales pages. They can come from a variety of outlets like mainstream media, prize award committees, and other influencers in your book's world and can be sourced in two ways: free and paid

Seek Free Editorial Reviews

First let's talk about free editorial reviews from influencers. There are three key steps to securing free editorial reviews.

---

1. Decide Who You Want on Your Cover

In your wildest dreams, who would you want to feature signing your book's praises? We might feel like we shouldn't ask the Margaret Atwoods or Jeff Bezos or whomever is the most famous guru relative to your reader audience, because, well, who are we, anyway?

What's the worst that can happen? Maybe they won't respond

to your request. Maybe they'll say no. Maybe they'll say yes! Include celebrities on your wish list when you really believe they'll have an interest in your book.

The point isn't to *expect* that your efforts will produce a celebrity review or even a response. It likely won't. But it's the *attitude*—the one that says me and my book are worth it—that counts.

So, with a big-blue-sky attitude, pinpoint your perfect endorser and then think in expanding concentric circles about similar people whose names you'd love to see next to an editorial review for your self-published book.

2. Find Those Who've Endorsed Similar Books

Now do a category search for books that are similar to yours or those you view as stretch competitors. Continuing from the theme above, don't limit yourself to books you deem to be of the same profile as yours. If your thriller will compete with Lee Child's *Jack Reacher* series, check his books for the editorial reviews. Make notes of who has reviewed them, whether they are affiliated with a particular organization, and in many cases you'll have to follow that with a bit of research about who each person is if it isn't already obvious.

3. Identify Influencers Related to Your Genre, Book, Industry, or Subject

If you're a nonfiction author, this could be a leader doing good work in the same or similar field, someone whose work you have quoted or cited, perhaps someone who has published a competing book. (Asking competitors is not verboten!) If you're a fiction author, this could be a leader of the community or region in which your novel is set, for example. In many of these cases, remember that with your aggressive marketing tactics there's an exposure benefit to these individuals. It's in their best interest.

What if they say no? It's fine, they will. You are not going to get 100 percent yeses but neither are you are unlikely to get 100 percent nos.

And when you purposefully go out and ask for editorial reviews for self-published books, good things happen. You might get an invitation to write a guest blog on a high-traffic blog site, or to be a guest on a podcast, or something else you already had on your book marketing to-do list anyway. It's a win-win.

Consider Paid Reviews

Paying for reviews is a controversial subject. However, there are different kinds of paid reviews. Some are quite reputable, provide an honest review, and may even be necessary in order to draw attention to your book—which otherwise might not be reviewed at all, as ALLi's Chief Watchdog, John Doppler, explains.

> Although there are several different types of reviews, most retailers distinguish between two clear-cut categories: customer reviews and editorial reviews. Customer reviews are informal reviews from customers, whereas editorial reviews are intended to be professional, unbiased, critical evaluations of a work by industry experts.
>
> Amazon applies different standards to each and separates the two kinds of reviews into their own sections to avoid confusion in the customer's mind. Of the two, Amazon uses a much lighter hand in policing editorial reviews; these can be added to the Editorial Reviews section of Author Central and are entirely under the control of the publisher.
>
> Additionally, there's the ethical concern of paying money to secure a supposedly unbiased customer review. With the exception of an advance reader copy of the book, any compensation offered to reviewers is a serious violation of Amazon's terms of service, whether that takes the form of direct payment, gift cards, credits, coupons, or other incentives.
>
> So which types of review services are acceptable? We can

divide review services into four major categories. Some are good, and some are a sure way to damage your career. All of them require caution.

Editorial Review Services

Reputable editorial review services rely on their reputation and experience to lend authority to their words. These are well-established organizations whose names are widely recognized, at least within the industry. A number of relatively newer services have also sprung up to cater to indie authors, and while these companies may not have the same caché as giants like the eighty-five-year-old Kirkus Reviews, they are slowly making a name for themselves in the industry.

A review that's dependent on the publisher's or author's money risks bias—or the *perception* of bias. Good editorial review services ensure the separation of the reviewer and the purchaser to eliminate that risk, and the best services are those with reputations for honest, objective reviews.

Paid editorial reviews from a reputable provider are ethical and are permitted by Amazon when confined to the Editorial Reviews section of a book's detail page. However, the value of these services to the indie author is endlessly debated. If you do choose to invest in an editorial review, you can find trusted, reputable service providers in our list of Best and Worst Self-Publishing Services.[1]

Matchmaker Services

Surprisingly, not all companies that offer customer reviews for a fee are an ethical lapse or a violation of retailers' rules. Matchmaker services fall into this slender zone of ethical paid review services.

Matchmaker services publicize a book to a list of interested reviewers, and so they're a closer cousin to marketing services than to reviewers.

As long as no compensation is offered to reviewers, and there are no expectations of a positive review or other restrictions placed on the reviewer, and reviewers are not reimbursed for purchases of the book, this practice does not violate Amazon's rules.

Unfortunately, it can be difficult to distinguish the honest services from the ethically compromised ones—especially if you happen to be an algorithm!

Even when legitimate, reviews originating from these services may attract unwanted attention from Amazon's screeners, and that could potentially lead to sweeping deletions of other reviews. Ethically, matchmaker services may pass muster, but in practice, they are fraught with danger.

Proxy Schemes

Proxy schemes attempt to circumvent rules against incentivized reviews by placing a middleman between the buyer and the reviewer. For example, the review service may pay reviewers for positive reviews, either with a gift card or direct payment. They may claim that this doesn't violate Amazon's rules because no money is changing hands between the author and the reviewer.

But that's sophistry. Compensating a reviewer is fundamentally dishonest, as the review is potentially compromised by the expectations of quid pro quo. Using a proxy is just as unethical as personally bribing the reviewer for a five-star review. The fact that you've paid an illicit service to do the dirty work on your behalf does not change the equation.

Also note that services that reimburse reviewers for the cost of the book are in direct violation of Amazon's Customer Review Guidelines. The guidelines explicitly prohibit this practice, as it's considered to be a fraudulent manipulation of the Verified Purchase badge. This may lead to deletion of your reviews, or even lead to termination of your Amazon account for fraud.

Avoid these services at all costs.

Fraudulent Review Services

At the far end of the review spectrum lie the "black hat" services, those which fabricate fake reviews for a fee. A hallmark of this kind of service is a guarantee of a large number of five-star reviews within a short time.

An honest review is dependent on the reviewer's personal taste and is inherently uncertain. Any service that guarantees a specific number of positive reviews is highly suspect.

It's Legal, Amazon Told Me So!

As a final note, and perhaps surprisingly to you, be wary of assurances that a company complies with all Amazon guidelines.

Amazon's customer support is notorious for giving contradictory answers, and all an unscrupulous service needs to do to acquire this facade of approval is to submit a question multiple times, or word it in a way that's unclear and open to interpretation. Eventually, they'll get a customer service representative who misunderstands the question and responds that it's okay.

One prominent service displays a response from Amazon stating that "you may go ahead with the advertising of the product," but doesn't disclose any correspondence leading up to this response. The client has no way of knowing what Amazon was told or if that discussion accurately reflects the nature of the service.

Rather than second-hand responses, ask the service provider for the exact method they're using to acquire reviewers and how those reviewers are compensated. Verify this information first-hand whenever possible. Look for other pages on the seller's website which invite people to become reviewers.

Do they promise compensation or reimbursement of costs? If so, the use of that service could land you in hot water.

The Bottom Line

Purchasing customer review services of any type is a risky proposition, one that ALLi's Watchdog Desk strongly discourages on both practical and ethical grounds. Editorial reviews are usually acceptable, but the guiding principle there should always be "buyer beware."

> Remember that it's your responsibility to ensure that you're using ethical services to promote your book. Do your homework, and steer clear of those services that sound too good to be true.
> They almost certainly are.
>
> — JOHN DOPPLER, ALLi WATCHDOG DESK

ALLi's Howard Lovy is the former executive editor at Foreword Reviews, where he was also in charge of Clarion Reviews, a fee-for-review service.

Lovy says that, under his watch, all paid reviews were objective and filled a need for many indie authors.

For Clarion Reviews, the fee simply assured those authors got a review. Good book or bad book, the fee paid for reviewers' and editors' time assured authors respectful treatment and consideration.

> There is a misconception that reviews in any publication are 'free.' What is supporting them is advertising revenue. This is true of *Foreword Reviews* and the *New York Times Book Review*. The traditional model is that advertising and subscription revenue offset the costs of printing the magazine or newspaper, paying the reviewers and editors, shipping the books, etc. So, the authors, themselves, are not paying, but somebody is. It's a model that worked well for more than a century, until recent years when declining ad and subscription revenue forced many magazines to either close down or severely cut back.
>
> — HOWARD LOVY, ALLi MULTIMEDIA MANAGER

Authors and publishers appreciate the opportunity to be reviewed by carefully chosen, professional review writers who provide a needed service.

Do your due diligence and ensure that if you decide to include paid reviews in your mix, you are selecting a reputable review service.

Key Takeaways

Paid and free editorial reviews can help with book sales, if you know the difference and follow the rules:

- Who would you love to endorse your book? Ask them, using the proper pitch formula.
- Reach out to reviewers who've endorsed books similar to yours.
- Show influencers related to your genre, industry, or subject that your marketing tactics will offer exposure for them.
- Paid reviews are controversial and must be done ethically .
- Using ARCs for a review can be considered a form of a paid review but is within Amazon's terms of service. Any other form of compensation is considered a violation.
- Reputable paid editorial review services separate the reviewer from the purchaser to avoid bias.
- Matchmaker services publicize books to a list of interested reviewers.
- Check ALLi's Watchdog Desk when considering a paid review service.
- ALLI's Watchdog strongly discourages purchasing customer review services of any type.

---

1. https://selfpublishingadvice.org/best-self-publishing-services/

7

BOOK BLOGGERS

Book bloggers are usually individuals who enjoy reading and reviewing, who sometimes gain financial rewards via affiliate links by promoting the books they review. But most book blogs are without profit motives or are produced by groups with a specific purpose, such as quality-assurance sites.

Book bloggers cultivate loyal readers and, as such, become trusted recommendation sources. Readers look to follow book bloggers who share their tastes in books, and that's one way they find new books they are likely to enjoy.

This trust gives book bloggers considerable power. Not surprisingly, book bloggers often find themselves sinking under the weight of ARCs from publishers because of their specialist readership. Publishers recognize that book bloggers are the most effective medium for reaching specific audiences.

The better and more influential a book blogger is, the more likely they are to be busy. Some book bloggers choose to reduce their load by refusing to review self-published books. This is like the bookstore proprietor who considers trade publishing as a seal of approval and quality control. If book bloggers have to reduce their to-read pile, that's one easy way to do it.

Your challenge is to customize your pitch to match the blogger's aims and convince them that they will love your book—and so will their readers.

The author of the influential Gav Reads blog gave the following reasons as to why a reviewer might choose not to read or review your self-published book:

- We don't know who you are.
- We don't know how you'll react.
- We'll feel guilty when we don't read it.
- We know you're not going to generate hits.
- We don't read cute bunny love stories set in Ancient Rome.
- We know it's going to be rubbish.

Not all book bloggers will be so explicit or feel so strongly. However, as a self-published author who is pitching a book to a blogger, you'll want to anticipate this sort of reaction so you can prepare to avoid potential objections.

Follow the tips we've already outlined in the chapter on "Getting Reviews" by:

- Ensuring you are pitching to the right book blogger.
- Keeping your pitch brief, professional, and to the point.
- Showing how the book blogger's readers will appreciate their review of your book.

Include the following information in any pitch to a book blogger:

- Your credentials as a high-quality author (e.g. your author website, previous media coverage, awards, and bestseller books).
- Existing positive reviews.
- Evidence of how you'll drive traffic to the blog or review outlet through your social media following.
- A professional information sheet about your book, showing title, jacket, categories, ISBN, publish date, copy from the

back cover or other brief summary, any relevant editorial review quotes or endorsements, your author photo and brief bio, your website URL, and your contact information.

Key Takeaways

When contacting book bloggers, remember:

- A recommendation by an influential book blogger offers great social proof for your book.
- Book bloggers are trusted sources with considerable power to boost a books interest and visibility.
- Best results happen when you customize your pitch to match the blogger's mission and audience.
- Pitch the right blogger, include the elements listed in this chapter, make your pitch brief, and tell your blogger how your book will benefit their audience.

8

MAINSTREAM MEDIA

Getting reviewed in mainstream (mass) media can feel like a major coup for an indie author. For the self-publishing community, it's also an encouraging indicator that high-profile platforms are willing to look less at how a book was published and more at what lies between their covers.

A single "worthy" line of praise from *The Washington Post* or *The Guardian* carries more weight with certain readers. Literary fiction, poetry and historical novels benefit most from these accolades, more so when they are also published in the newspapers that offered the endorsements because of the sway they have over their readers.

Not only that – traditional reviews can also prove beneficial in marketing campaigns, converting more browsers into readers because of the empirical sense of social proof associated with an endorsement from a recognisable brand name. You can use them in Facebook ads, of course, but also on advanced information sheets – a document that you can give to librarians and bookstore managers to help get your books stocked on their shelves. In this circumstance, it's not the content of the review that carries the weight, more the name attached to it that proves invaluable.

Media reviews are sometimes called "editorial reviews" or "endorsements", and authors who receive glowing comments often showcase them on front covers, inside the front matter, and on their online pages. Such reviews don't all have to come from mainstream media review outlets. In this chapter we'll discuss where else you might source them.

When you are considering the value of mainstream media in your reviews strategy, bear in mind that editors and reviewers on these book pages are, like book bloggers, inundated with ARCs. They also have a long-standing and close relationship with trade-publishing houses who have been providing them with great books for decades, and who may also pay for the ads that keep the review pages going. They therefore have far more clout than you.

The value of mass media publicity isn't as easy to assess as the online initiatives we've already discussed. Firstly, it isn't usually directly about sales. It's about growing and strengthening your author platform. That may well be worthwhile for you. Good editorial reviews improve your sales pages, your website and your overall reach and make you and your books more attractive to readers. But be honest with yourself, wearing your publisher, not your author, hat. This can easily become a vanity exercise. If you are putting all your efforts into mass media outlets for poor return, while less prestigious niche reviewers and bloggers with a following in your genre give better results, you might need to rethink your strategy.

With digital marketing and advertising campaigns, price promotions, and email marketing, you can easily see and compare the results of your efforts.

Self-published authors, without an existing relationship with media outlets, and who may be on such a small budget that they have to think twice about whether they can afford to dispatch a complimentary print copy, simply cannot compete with mainstream publishers in this arena.

As a guiding rule, stick to electronic copies and don't send a physical review copy unless it has specifically been requested. And put your efforts where you are most likely to glean results, especially at first.

Delve into Features, Editorials, and Opinion Sections

Look beyond the Books or Arts or Culture sections of any major newspaper or publication to find the feature pages, the editorials, and the opinion sections. There you will find opportunities to connect with a much wider range of readers and these pages are far more open to self-published authors than the review pages.

When a book makes this crossover, readers of the article stop thinking about it simply as a book and start seeing it as essential further reading about issues that are central to their lives.

This approach works particularly well for nonfiction or for high-concept fiction and non-fiction with unusual themes or approaches.

Self-published books, being free of the bounds and rules of trade-publishing houses, might be seen as the natural home of more thought-provoking topics and therefore the first place that feature editors look for such material. If you have a story to tell and an unusual angle to offer in your well-selling book, consider actively seeking opportunities for reviews, recommendation columns, or feature coverage in mainstream media and their respective special sections.

Clearly spell out the news angle or feature idea to the appropriate section editor.

Go Local

Local news outlets are always on the lookout for a local angle or local story. Look close to home, and see how you might gain coverage and build a reputation with regional media, print, TV, or radio, where there is an ongoing need for locally available commentators and experts. Local broadcasts and periodicals generally have a much smaller staff and are more accessible than national media.

Approaching your local paper or lifestyle magazine is usually more affordable and practical for the self-published author than competing for the top national spots. Local audiences tend to feel more ownership and connection with local authors, which may also translate into higher sales and readership of your book.

To increase your chance of having your book accepted for a local spot or media feature, always include in your application the items listed in the "Getting Reviews" and "Book Bloggers" chapters.

Understand the Gatekeeper Role

ALLi's Howard Lovy spent the first part of his career as a journalist and has some tips on how an author can get the attention of a local newspaper.

I've spent my career as a gatekeeper, making decisions about who is newsworthy, which person has the expertise, credibility, and connection with my audience to be worth interviewing. Because many news releases cross my path every day, most of these decisions need to be split-second and, perhaps, unfair. However, there are ways to increase the chance that a member of the media will want to care.

Be Local

One of the first words I learned as a reporter was localization. Local media (TV, radio, print, online) are all looking for their own take on a national or international story.

A conflict flares up in a foreign country, and you've written a travel memoir about how you hiked through the countryside and got to know the land and people before the disturbance. The national media won't necessarily talk to you since they have a world of experts and boots on the ground from which to draw. Your local media will, if you emphasize immediately that you are local and have something important to contribute to the debate.

You're not hawking your book right away. The fact that you have just released a book on the topic, though, gives your story just one more news hook that might tip the scales for an editor or reporter.

Be Relevant

Make the right pitch to the right publication. Tailor your news release. This takes more time, but it is worth it. "Local" is not necessarily confined to physical location. Local can simply mean "relevant." There are communities that are tied together by interest but are physically scattered around the world.

Is there a local community that would be interested in your book? Odds are, there are publications devoted to it. Local is how you build your brand initially and establish credibility within your own community. After that's done, after you can show that you've been quoted, interviewed, and sourced as an expert on your topic, then you can move on to the big leagues to see if you can get the attention of the *New York Times* or *Good Morning America*.

Be Newsy

Stay alert to what's happening in the news right now. What is trending? What issues are being discussed on Sunday morning talk shows? Is there a bill pending in Congress or your parliament that will address an issue you discuss in your book? Was there a recent news event in the country you write about? Has a celebrity recently revealed he or she suffers from a condition you cover in your book?

Be careful, though. There is a fine line between opportunism and exploitation. A few authors were heavily mocked and criticized on social media for using Robin Williams' suicide as an excuse to draw attention to themselves. Be sensitive. It's not about you. It's about the topic with which you have expertise.

This is not only confined to nonfiction, of course. If pitched correctly, your novel can find a news hook. Does your novel raise an issue that goes beyond your book? Does it question assumptions? Does it rethink a historical figure? Does it feature a dilemma that is universal? Is it in a genre that is being discussed in the larger literary world? For example, YA that is also enjoyed by adults? Are you donating a percentage of the proceeds of your book to a charity you believe in? Does your book deal with drug addiction, for example, so you'd like to donate a percentage to a local rehab center?

These elements, especially ones that seem counterintuitive, will get the media's attention.

Be Quick

Cut to the chase. From the very first sentence of your news release, there needs to be information you are certain an editor would be interested in. Odds are, nobody is going to even get to the second paragraph of your release (or even the subject line of your email). Place yourself in the shoes of the editor or reporter you're pitching to, think of what she will likely be most interested in, and dive in directly.

So, as you pitch coverage of your book, you'll be frustrated, you'll feel unfairly ignored, you'll need to try many different tactics. But if you keep these general rules in mind, you'll find that the media will care about you. And, through news coverage, perhaps everybody will care about your book.

— HOWARD LOVY, ALLI's MULTIMEDIA MANAGER

Key Takeaways

When seeking reviews or articles or stories in the Media, News, and Features, keep in mind:

- Mass media reviews aren't for everyone, but are most useful if you have front-of-shop distribution in brick-and-mortar stores.
- Media publicity isn't directly about sales…it's about the opportunity to *achieve* sales.
- Features, editorials, and opinion pieces are a natural home for more thought-provoking topics of self-published authors.
- Clearly pitch the current news angle or feature idea to the appropriate sections' editor.
- Go local…whether with a local angle (such as location), a

local story (such as an event that resembles a theme or storyline in your book), or a local store that features local authors.
- Use the right hook to make the right pitch to the right publication/section/editor focusing on the news right now.

9

USING GOODREADS

Goodreads is the social media platform for readers. There, readers search for books, read reviews, participate in group discussions, and chat to other readers. It's also a social cataloguing site that allows users to register books they've written or read and create reading lists and challenges. There are also all kinds of lists and polls, which some enjoy and others abhor due to their susceptibility to being influenced by popular authors with large platforms. The practice results in dubious rankings where books by living authors are placed above classical authors who, long dead, can't mobilize their fans to take part.

Some authors swear by Goodreads as a great place for writers to bond with readers, share book recommendations, and participate in discussions. Others fight shy, disliking that the platform is owned by Amazon, resenting the lack of investment in the site (it's clunky and old-fashioned) and feeling that Goodreads reviewers are less forgiving than those on other platforms.

Although Goodreads is owned by Amazon, but its rules and standards are different. A reviewer writing about the same book on both sites will generally give one fewer star on Goodreads than on

Amazon due to the different standards for their respective star systems.

Goodreads, as the name implies, is a site for *readers*. As an author, you can use Goodreads to reach readers and garner reviews, but if you are pushy, readers will push back, with a vengeance.

Whether you love of hate Goodreads, it's hard to argue that it is not influential, given that 50 million readers are there, on that single platform. Getting reviews there can help an author sell more books and grow a loyal fanbase.

In this chapter, we will explore six ways you can use the platform to get your books noticed, expand your reach on Goodreads, and generate more reviews on the platform, with help from social media expert and ALLi Goodreads Moderator, Barb Drozdowich. "In my mind, the power of networking on Goodreads is only limited by my creativity. Unlike Facebook or Twitter, you don't have to ask account holders if they read—just *what* they read. And while I don't believe that Goodreads is the only place that you should network, it should be part of your efforts."

1. Goodreads Shelves

Goodreads allows an account holder to list the books that they have read or want to read. They are supplied with some default shelves as well as the ability to create as many custom shelves as they want. Every time you as a reader or an account holder list a book on a shelf, that information is shared with all of your friends. Like Amazon or Facebook, Goodreads is controlled by algorithms, so putting books on certain shelves is more important than other shelves.

The idea behind shelves is not just an organizational tool, it is a sharing vehicle. It helps you share with other people. I'm sure you're not nosy, but lots of people are interested in what other people are doing. They are curious as to what books their friends are reading. They may choose friends based on their taste in books. Every time you log in to your Goodreads account, you are shown what your friends are doing, reading, and reviewing.

If you want to put your author hat back on, consider how much free advertising you can give your author friends by listing their books on a shelf of yours, perhaps by reviewing it. Consider creating a shelf called "Great Authors." List all your friends' books on the shelf. People will notice.

2. Goodreads Friends/Followers

I consider the connection between people on Goodreads to be its second most important functionality.

On Goodreads, people can be *friends* of one another. This is an action that one person requests and the receiver accepts. In addition, readers can be *followers* of authors. This is a one-sided interaction started by the reader; it does not need to be accepted by the author.

These two types of interactions have different powers.

Although on Goodreads authors are encouraged to increase the number of followers, I believe both groups have importance. An author profile on Goodreads comes with quite a bit of functionality that many authors don't seem to know about.

One of my favorites is connecting an author's blog to Goodreads via the RSS feed. This not only allows people to read blog posts on Goodreads, but also to get email notification whenever a new post is created by Goodreads.

I have over 300 more readers of my blog than are visible from my blog stats because those are followers on Goodreads.

On the main landing page of Goodreads is what's called the newsfeed. This allows readers to keep up-to-date with what their friends are doing. You may not spend much time scanning this information, but many people do. I have well over 3,000 friends who are aware of a wide variety of things that I do on Goodreads, such as put a book on a shelf, add a book to a reading challenge, or enter a giveaway.

It's not uncommon for me to be notified of somebody else marking a book that I've just finished sharing as 'to read.' Likely they caught sight of it on their newsfeed.

3. Goodreads Giveaways

Do we as authors give away copies of our books in hopes of getting reviews? Obviously, the answer to that question is yes. Do we always get reviews? Sadly, the answer to that question is no—but we hope. There are two main positive things about the Goodreads giveaways:
—the potential for reviews
—the placement on shelves.

We always hope that every book we give away for a review will get us a review. When giving away a book on Goodreads, stack the deck in your favor. You are given the name of the winner, so write them a nice letter asking for a review and explaining how to do it. I typically write a short note in the book, not on a separate piece of paper. Can these books be found for sale on Amazon or eBay? Yes, of course, but then perhaps the next person will review the book as well.

Don't focus on the money spent; focus on the possibility of a review and of the networking potential.

The second point that is overlooked is the shelf aspect. When a reader enters a Goodreads giveaway, the book is automatically placed on their 'to-read' shelf and this information is shared with all of their friends. To avoid this second step, people have to uncheck a box.

To remove the book from their shelves, they have to go to the trouble of actually deleting.

Typically, these books will stay on shelves as a constant reminder to the reader that they had expressed interest in a book. It also serves as a reminder to their friends that they have an interest in this book.

These giveaways attract a lot of attention. On average, 825 people enter a giveaway and over 40,000 people enter multiple giveaways each day on Goodreads.

That's a heck of a lot of attention for the cost of a book and postage.

4. Goodreads Groups

Groups are often considered to be the shining star of Goodreads. Many of my fellow book bloggers seem to live in their groups. There are many groups whose only function seems to be authors announcing a book release or a book for sale, but the real networking power of groups is found in the other groups.

For example, did you realize that there are upwards of 10,000 book clubs that have groups on Goodreads?

There are groups from every geographical area of the world, covering every genre of book and, in fact, all sorts of non-book subjects.

Are you interested in finding some friends and readers on the other side of the world from where you live? I bet there's a group from that country—whichever country that might be.

How about a group that talks about things you're interested in other than books? Great way to make online friends.

Most of the groups allow their members to create a profile or an introduction. All of the books that you have written as an author are attached to your profile.

Let's face it, we readers aren't stupid. If we want to buy a book, we know how.

5. Goodreads Reading Challenges

The reading challenge functionality, I think, is one of the most overlooked functions on Goodreads. It allows readers to decide arbitrarily how many books they are going to read in a calendar year. It then allows the readers to record the books that they read as well as ratings or reviews.

Just like with shelves, every time a book is recorded as being read, that information is shared with the reader's friends. It is also part of the reading challenge list.

Anybody can go into someone's list and comment or just look at the books on the list. In addition to that, readers can advertise that they are doing a reading challenge on the sidebar of their blog.

One thing I encourage authors to do is create a shelf called *reading challenge*, then use the widget functionality to display what they've been reading on the sidebar of their blog. In fact, authors can get together and be rather strategic about what books are displaying.

I've done a reading challenge several times. I've found there has been a lot of interaction between people who are doing the challenge. Quite a few of the books that I've read in the last calendar year have been added to other people's shelves. Again, not flashy, but networking.

6. Goodreads Events

The event notification on Goodreads can be overused, but on the other hand it is an easy way to communicate with all your friends. It allows you to divide the audience. For example, if I were going to have an in-person event, I could invite people based on their geography. But think about the power: every time I have a book release, I have over 3,000 people to share this information with. That is in addition to the number on my mailing list. Quiet, yet powerful.

Key Takeaways

With fifty million readers, Goodreads is a worthwhile platform to explore when looking to connect with new readers and collect reviews. We've offered six different networking opportunities that can help you get reviews on Goodreads:

- Place your book on the virtual shelves.
- Connect your blog's RSS feed to Goodreads and connect with friends and followers.
- Consider Goodreads giveaways to increase the potential for reviews and for placement on shelves.
- Harness the networking power of groups, like one of the 10,000 book clubs' groups, geographic groups, or genre.
- Create a shelf called "reading challenge," then use the widget functionality to display what you've been reading on the sidebar of your blog.
- Use the event notification on Goodreads to announce the release of your new books.

10

RESPONDING TO REVIEWS

We will all get negative reviews at some point in our indie author journey, no matter how great we think our books are. Indeed, some writers even see it as a badge of honor to receive a savage one-star, because it demonstrates to the world that your reviewers aren't all friends and relations. But that doesn't stop it from hurting, at least for a little while—especially if the reason for the review feels unfair.

At the time of this writing, as we discussed in the chapter "Amazon Reviews," there is an option on Amazon to vote a review *helpful* or *unhelpful*. Some marketers advise you to rally your friends and supporters to vote favorable reviews helpful, keeping the positive reviews at the top and pushing the less favorable reviews down the page.

Whether you do this or not comes down to your own conscience.

Others dislike this kind of behavior, thinking it smacks of desperation as well as a disregard for the ability of the reader to judge reviews and make up their mind accordingly. Customer reviews are supposed to be customer reviews.

Don't Respond

When you receive a bad review, the only appropriate response is silence. No matter how ridiculous or undeserved the review, you must rise above it.

Responding with a defensive retort or rallying your friends to defend your book on your behalf is the hallmark of an inexperienced author who does not understand the etiquette of the marketplace. Keep your gaze high and disregard any slight.

If the poor review is truly unjust and undeserved, discerning readers will spot its flaws without any assistance, just as most people can see straight through the gushing praise of a book written by the author's best friend.

Do not respond. If you do, you risk getting into a damaging verbal boxing match over which you have no control. Pick a fight with a troll —and there are plenty of weirdos out there who really are spoiling for such a fight—and you will only make the situation worse. Just walk away, get a cup of coffee, and move on with the more important things in your day (which is everything else).

You have little control over reviews posted online other than to request removal of any that are defamatory or clearly inappropriate, if it's clear the reviewer hasn't read the book but is complaining about a delivery delay or other grievance, or the review is offensive.

Concentrate on the positive.

Learn What You Can from Constructive Criticism

Too many authors take umbrage at three-star reviews. Three stars is still positive!

Consider whether you have lost a star for a particular issue, such as typos. In which case, the only appropriate response is silence. You want to rise above it and take the chance to put it right. In this case, it would be getting your book proofread.

Over time, as you digest bad reviews, you may start to realize the negative reviewer was doing you a favor by pointing out a valid issue. Constructive criticism can really help you grow as an author—

although of course we'd all prefer if it came privately pre-publication, from good editors or beta readers. (Might you benefit from starting to use beta readers or adding more of them to your process?)

Of course, if all your reviews are one-star, maybe you need to think again about the quality of what you are putting out there—but I've yet to see any book get that treatment.

Most authors get largely three, four, or five stars, with a smattering of one and two stars, usually from people who the book just wasn't right for.

And if you're getting a lot of those, consider whether you're marketing your book to the wrong audience, with inappropriate cover art, blurb, categories, etc.

Consider the Context

While ignoring a bad review isn't always easy, setting it into context will help you gain a sense of perspective. You can often diminish its sting by clicking on the reviewer's profile to see what else they've been up to.

On a review describing your book as "the worst book I've ever read," written by someone who has never reviewed any other book, you can be sure they are a troll with nothing better to do. "More to be pitied than blamed," as my kindly grandmother used to say.

If you have a poor review of a sweet romance by someone who only ever gives five stars to vampire novels, you can be pretty sure they're not the best judge of your genre.

If a one-star comes from someone who gives five stars only to household cleaning products and clothing for dogs, you can be equally sure they're not the best judge of books.

Adopt my favorite strategy: mentally award the same number of stars to your reviewer as they've given to your book. What, got a one-star review? It's clearly from a one-star reader (poor soul)!

And don't jump to the conclusion that a one-star review is going to be terrible. Surprisingly often reviewers will click the wrong star button and give a low rating to a book they say they absolutely loved!

The Only Time You Should Take Action

If the criticism has nothing to do with your book, e.g. "did not arrive" or "not what I ordered," then that is according to Amazon's Terms and Conditions an unfair review of your work. Message Amazon to report it, and if you're lucky, they will remove it. But if they don't, it's not the end of the world—anyone reading it won't think less of you as an author or of your book for it.

Put Yourself in the Reader's Position

In all of this, remember you are looking at this review as the author—and the book is your baby. Readers see it differently. You will read between the lines, over-analyze, and take each word to heart. Readers will just be casting their eye over a few reviews and may not even read them in full.

If they're a serious potential customer for your book, they won't be put off by the odd crazy, and they'll be smart enough to realize which reviews are credible. Besides, a surprising number of book buyers never read reviews at all, but buy because of your beautiful cover, carefully crafted blurb, skillful marketing, outstanding reputation. So, the significance of reviews in the buying process may be less crucial than it might seem.

Glass Half-Full

Finally, focus on the positives. I'm betting that for every less-than-fabulous review, you have plenty that you're proud of. Those are the ones you should read and reread, and pin on the wall over your desk, and share on your social media and website to wring every last drop of pride out of the praise.

And if that still doesn't do it for you, then take this piece of advice from ALLi Director Orna Ross: "Get as many reviews as you ethically can—but ideally don't read them! Or, if you do, try not to take them too seriously, the good or the bad."

Responding to Good Reviews

When you receive a great review, spread the word via social media. Tweet a link, post it on Facebook, or use other social media to hint to other readers that they may like to follow suit.

There are ways you can make these reviews work harder for you. First, quote favorable reviews in your marketing materials, on your author website, or as endorsements on future publications.

Favorable reviews are also very useful when promoting your book elsewhere, for example when trying to get it stocked in a bricks-and-mortar store.

Even though discerning people will recognize that all good reviews are objective, it's certainly helpful to be able to cite plenty of online stars as social proof of your book's worth.

Key Takeaways

When responding to reviews, simpler is better:

- Get as many reviews as you ethically can, then don't take them too seriously.
- Know that undeserved negative reviews are easily recognized by readers for what they are.
- Don't respond to a negative review with defensiveness or rally friends to respond on your behalf.
- Do ask for a negative review to be removed if it defamatory or clearly inappropriate, such as a delayed delivery (knowing your request may or may not be granted).
- Learn from constructive criticism instead of fretting about it. Reviews are feedback…take it in your stride. Work hard on the aspects you control: your beautiful cover, book description, marketing.
- Decide on your position regarding the helpful or unhelpful button on Amazon to increase positive reviews visibility in the algorithm.

- Respond to good reviews by spreading the news via social media and your email list.

11

NEXT STEPS

Ready to take action? Here's a list of steps you can take to gain honest and ethical reviews for your book. Remember, there is not one single, best way to get reviews. Make your own decisions about what is the best approach for you and your book.

1. **PLAN**. Plan early. Distribute printed pre-publication copies to readers to garner early reviews and quotable quotes. Don't enroll in Kindle Unlimited until after you've finished distributing your ARCs.
2. Make a list of the celebrities, influencers, and podcasters who you would most like to review your book.
3. Make a list of those who have endorsed other books in your genre, subject, or category.
4. Make a list of reviewers and book bloggers in your genre, subject, category.
5. **PITCH**. Make your pitch: Write any or all of the people on your lists and ask for a review. Follow ALLi's ethical code, be brief, show how your book is a benefit to their audience.
6. Engage in Goodreads, using virtual bookshelves, giveaways,

networking groups, reading challenges, and event notifications.
7. Take advantage of a timely event and localize it. Pitch the local angle as it relates to your book to local newspapers, feature editors, local news broadcasts, the features section.
8. **ASK**. Ask for reviews in the back of your own books. Ask for reviews in marketing materials, book clubs, speaking engagements, and on Goodreads.
9. Suggest reviews be left on the platforms where your book appears. Provide targeted links to the review pages of where you want to review to appear, be it on Goodreads, BookBub, Kobo, Barnes & Noble, Apple Books, Amazon, and even your own website.
10. **SHARE**. Show your appreciation…say thank you, in person or via private messaging, in emails, handwritten notes or across social media.
11. Share your reviews in public, on your website, on your author pages, and on social media.
12. **REPEAT**. Continue with this process for the life of your book to encourage more visibility, social proof, and consistent sales.

And now, taking our own advice: It would mean the world to the team here at ALLi if you would take a moment to post a review on the platform where you obtained this book.

Thank you!

APPENDIX: ETHICAL AUTHOR CODE
ALLIANCE OF INDEPENDENT AUTHORS

Guiding Principle: Putting the Reader First

When I market my books, I put my readers first. This means that I don't engage in any practices that have the effect of misleading the readers/buyers of my books. I behave professionally both online and offline when it comes to the following practices in my writing life:

Courtesy

I behave with courtesy and respect toward readers, other authors, reviewers, and industry professionals such as agents and publishers. If I find myself in disagreement, I focus on issues rather than on airing grievances or complaints in the press or online. Engaging in personal attacks is totally out of the question.

Aliases

I don't hide behind an alias to boost my own sales or to damage the sales or reputation of another person. If I adopt a pen name for legitimate reasons, I use it consistently and carefully.

Reviewing and Rating Books

I don't review or rate my own or another author's books in any way that misleads or deceives the reader. I am transparent about my relationships with other authors when reviewing their books.

I'm transparent about any reciprocal reviewing arrangements and avoid any practices that could result in the reader being deceived.

Reacting to Reviews

I don't react to any book review by harassing the reviewer, getting a third party to harass the reviewer, or making any form of intrusive contact with the reviewer. If I've been the subject of a personal attack in a review, I respond in a way that is consistent with professional behavior.

Book Promotions

I don't promote my books by making false statements about, for example, their position on bestseller lists. I don't consent to anyone else promoting them for me in a misleading manner.

Plagiarism

I know that plagiarism is a serious matter, and I don't intentionally try to pass off another writer's words as my own.

Financial Ethics

In my business dealings as an author, I make every effort to be accurate and prompt with payments and financial calculations. If I have made a financial error, I remedy it as soon as it's brought to my notice.

Responsibility

I take responsibility for how my books are sold and marketed. If I learn that anyone is acting against the spirit or letter of this Code on my behalf, I will refer them to this Code and insist that they modify their behavior.

You can download your Ethical Author badge here[1] and display it on your author website.

Reviewing Rules

Every bookselling platform will have rules, or guidelines, about "legal" reviews.

Here is an excerpt from the rules for Amazon customer reviews.

> Authors are welcome to submit Customer Reviews, unless the reviewing author has a personal relationship with the author of the book being reviewed or was involved in the book's creation process (i.e., as a co-author, editor, illustrator, etc.). If so, that author isn't eligible to write a Customer Review for that book.
>
> — Amazon Customer Reviews

So, you cannot:

- Self-review your books.
- Get your mom (or any family member) to post an Amazon review.
- Pay someone to write a customer review of your book.
- Post a customer review on behalf of somebody else.

You can:

- Review the books of other authors, as long as you don't have

a personal relationship with them and you did not help write or publish their book.
- Complain to Amazon if you think a review is inappropriate.

Research the reviewing rules for each of the platforms where you intend to sell or are selling your book(s).

---

1. https://selfpublishingadvice.org/alli-campaigns/ethical-author/

THE END

ACKNOWLEDGMENTS

All good books are a team effort. An author's name goes on the cover but behind that is the creative team of editors and designers and formatters who made the book, the distributors and marketers who take it to readers, and the long list of supporters—from family members to work colleagues—without whom it would never have been created.

Then there are the other writers, from journalists and academics to storytellers and poets, who have published relevant ideas, information and inspirations that, quite literally, underwrite the book.

All this is true for this book you hold in your hand and our thanks to all those who had a hand in its making.

Thanks are due to all at the Alliance of Independent Authors (ALLi). ALLi guides rely heavily on the work and wisdom of our team, members, ambassadors and advisors. All of this is generously and freely shared with our non-profit CIC (Community Interest Company), with the intention of paying it forward, and benefitting other indie authors. Thank you for your generosity and for lighting the way.

For this guide to *Your First 50 Book Reviews*, particular thanks are due to ALLi team members and blog contributors: Dorah Blume, John

Doppler, Barb Drozdowich, Dan Holloway, Mark Horrell, Dan Parsons, Russell Phillips, Orna Ross, Boni Wagner Stafford, and Debbie Young.

JOIN ALLI

Alliance of Independent Authors

ALLi, the Alliance of Independent Authors is the global association for self-publishing indie authors.

Join us for reliable advice and advocacy, discounts, free guidebooks and resources, member forums, contract review, motivation, education and support from a wonderful indie author community.

AllianceIndependentAuthors.org

facebook.com/AllianceIndieAuthors
twitter.com/indieauthoralli

MORE ADVICE & FEEDBACK

ADVICE UPDATES FROM ALLI

Would you like to receive a monthly roundup of self-publishing advice from our award-winning blog?

Write more books. Reach more readers. Sell more Books.
Sign up for ALLi updates
Direct to your inbox each Wednesday

WE'D LOVE YOUR FEEDBACK
REVIEW REQUEST

If you enjoyed this book, would you consider leaving a brief review online on your favorite online bookstore that takes reviews: Amazon, Apple, Barnes and Noble Goodreads or Kobo?

A good review is very important to authors these days as it helps other readers know this is a book worth their time.

It doesn't have to be long or detailed. Just a sentence saying what you enjoyed and a star-rating is all that's needed. Many thanks.

Your First 50 Book Reviews
COPYRIGHT © ALLIANCE OF INDEPENDENT AUTHORS | 2021

EBOOK: 978-1-913349-70-7
PAPERBACK: 978-1-913349-71-4
LARGE PRINT: 978-1-913349-81-3

THE AUTHORS'S MORAL RIGHTS HAVE BEEN ASSERTED. ALL RIGHTS RESERVED. ENQUIRIES: INFO@ORNAROSS.COM

Created with Vellum

www.ingramcontent.com/pod-product-compliance
Lightning Source LLC
Chambersburg PA
CBHW021128080526
44587CB00012B/1191